M000036348

Marilyn Schrock not only knows what she is writing about but she also is not afraid to write what she knows. The Bible says, "My people are destroyed for lack of knowledge" (Hosea 6:4). Jesus himself said, "You shall know the truth and the truth shall make you free" (John 8:32). I believe many people will be set free as they learn the truth about astral projection. The miracle you have been praying for may be the very book you hold in your hands.

—APOSTLE BOBBY HOGAN
BOBBY HOGAN MINISTRIES
CHRIST FOR THE WORLD INTERNATIONAL
FT. SMITH, ARKANSAS

This book by Marilyn Schrock makes me aware of what has secretly plagued the church and Christians for years. This message empowers us to know about and overcome satan's strongholds.

—ROBERTA THOMSON, D.D.
INTERCESSOR AND CO-PASTOR
POTTER'S HANDS CHURCH
EMPORIA, KANSAS

My husband and I have been in ministry together forty-four years. We met Marilyn Schrock thirty years ago, and we have been close in the Spirit with her all these years. This book is full of God's wisdom and revelation about astral projection and how to overcome it. We only wish we could have had this knowledge years ago.

We know we have the power to overcome all the works of the devil. This book is an eye-opener because it gives details of the enemy camp and tells us how to specifically and with precise aim destroy the devil's stronghold of astral projection. Marilyn Schrock brings God's light into the devil's great deception and darkness of astral projection and shows us how to overcome it.

We believe every church, pastor, intercessor, ministry leader and believer needs the message in this book so they can identify those held captive, set the captives free, and bring the kingdom of God to the earth as it is in heaven (Matt. 6:10).

—PASTORS RALPH AND JUDY ABLIN
FAITH COMMUNITY CHURCH
SEGUIN, TEXAS

WAKE UP, CHURCH!

THE ENEMY IS WITHIN
YOUR GATES

MARILYN SCHROCK

CREATION HOUSE
A STRANG COMPANY

WAKE UP, CHURCH! THE ENEMY IS WITHIN YOUR GATES!
by Marilyn Schrock
Published by Creation House
A Strang Company
600 Rinehart Road
Lake Mary, Florida 32746
www.strangbookgroup.com

Unless otherwise noted, all Scripture quotations are from the New King James Version of the Bible. Copyright © 1979, 1980, 1982 by Thomas Nelson, Inc., publishers. Used by permission.

Scripture quotations marked KJV are from the King James Version of the Bible.

English definitions are from *Webster's New World Dictionary*, 2nd College Edition, 1982.

Publisher's Note: The views expressed in this book are not necessarily the views held by the publisher.

Design Director: Bill Johnson
Cover design by Amanda Potter

Library of Congress Control Number: 2009927902
International Standard Book Number: 978-1-59979-852-3

First Edition

09 10 11 12 13 — 9 8 7 6 5 4 3 2 1
Printed in the United States of America

DEDICATION

This book is gratefully dedicated to my Lord Jesus Christ who has preserved my life, soul, and spirit and to Rev. Roberta Thomson, His servant and friend and my partner in ministry, who has provided love, prayers, and shelter so I could write this book. She has opened her heart and home to me and to Kevin; together we have founded The Potter's Hands and ventured forth on mission trips and exploits to Jamaica. We have been in awe of the Lord and of His mighty works, signs, and wonders on our journeys together.

For certain men have crept in unnoticed.
—Jude 4

CONTENTS

ACKNOWLEDGMENTS

I WISH TO EXPRESS MY HEARTFELT THANKS TO THOSE precious saints of God who have supported me through their prayers and substance to allow me to give myself wholly to prayer and to the ministry of the Word.

This book would not be possible without those precious saints who risked all to share their personal stories with me. As the church has been awakened to the projectors around us, many saints have stepped forward with stories they feared would not be believed. At first they were timid, but as more and more people began to open up and share their deepest secrets, we strengthened each other and learned by the leading of the Holy Spirit of a secret and unseen enemy that was harassing the body of Christ.

I deeply love and appreciate each one of the precious saints who has contributed to this book. Without their help and much prayer and strengthening by the Holy Spirit, this book could not have been written.

In January and February of 2008 the Lord brought a pastor from Jamaica to be our guest. He shared a wealth of information about astral projection with us. We took him to Engeltal at Jasper, Arkansas, to speak to the leadership at End Time Handmaidens personally. It was a greatly anointed time together with the Holy Spirit.

More than two years before that meeting in her home at Engeltal, Sister Gwen Shaw had looked me in the eye and said to me, "You know a lot about astral projection and the Lord wants you to write an article about it." How did she know?

It was a secret and struggle my church and I had been dealing with for several years. With this assignment to write about it, new help came, and the Holy Spirit strengthened me and gave me understanding and revelation. This book tells about how the secret enemy works, how to defeat it, how to overcome it, and how to deliver the projector.

FOREWORD

Marilyn Schrock's book on astral projection contains a much-needed message, because very little is written on this important subject. The church has very little understanding of the dangers connected with this demonic supernatural activity, and therefore many zealous souls who are seeking for the miraculous can get ensnared by Satan.

Astral projection is Satan's imitation of biblical translation, such as happened to Philip in the early church. Many true Christians have been translated by the power of God to bear witness for Him. Enoch and Elijah were translated to heaven without seeing death. Church history has many accounts, both in the Vatican and since the Reformation, of sincere Christians who have been translated.

What, then, is the difference? One is good, and the other is evil. To obtain this power, one must be "sold out" to God, or to Satan. Satan does not give these powers to just anyone. Satan has powerful religious spirits that have at times deceived even the elect.

When I was in Africa, I met an African preacher who had been a powerful witch. He had "sold his soul" to Satan in order to obtain power to do miracles, such as astral projection. He told me he could astral project himself all over the world in a moment of time. He had obtained this power by killing his only son when he was still a very young child. Sad to say, Satan does not easily let go of his bondslaves. This preacher fell back into sin and died a mysterious death.

This book is a warning to all. Do not play with fire! You will get burnt! You don't want anything the devil has to offer! On the other hand, don't reject the truly miraculous mysteries of God just because the devil is a good imitator of the real.

If you are not living a holy life, don't desire to have the power to do miracles. Holiness and the love of the Word of God are of more value than signs and wonders. The multitudes who followed Jesus fell away because they would have rather seen signs and wonders than heard the oracles of God that came out of His mouth.

Read this book and share it with your children and grandchildren. Our youth need to be warned. Give it to your Christian friends. The church needs to wake up before it is too late!

—GWEN R. SHAW
FOUNDER, END-TIME HANDMAIDENS, INC.

Chapter 1

WHAT IS ASTRAL PROJECTION?

*Be sober, be vigilant; because your adversary
the devil walks about like a roaring lion,
seeking whom he may devour.*

—1 Peter 5:8

SATAN IS THE FATHER OF LIES AND A DECEIVER (John 8:44). If possible, he would deceive even the elect (Mark 13:22). He uses the believing of lies in the minds of men to hold them in bondage. "But evil men and impostors will grow worse and worse, deceiving and being deceived" (2 Tim. 3:13). The book of Revelation indicates that all of the lost were deceived.

Second Corinthians 11:13–15 tells us:

> For such are false apostles, deceitful workers, transforming themselves into apostles of Christ. And no wonder! For Satan himself transforms himself into an angel of light. Therefore it is no great thing if his ministers also transform

themselves into ministers of righteousness, whose end will be according to their works.

Our enemy works in stealth mode, an enemy we can't see. His deception goes deeper and further than most Christians believe or even imagine. "The thief does not come except to steal, and to kill, and to destroy" (John 10:10). The devil does not have the power to create. He can only counterfeit what the Lord has already created. For example, in Acts 8:39–40 it tells of a time when the Lord transported Philip (body, soul, and spirit) from one place to another. The enemy has counterfeited this with astral projection, which involves the spirit and soul of a person.

Astral projection is also known as astral travel, endless traveler, or out-of-body experiences.[1] To understand astral projection, one must realize the Lord created each person to have three parts to their being:

- a physical body
- a soul (mind, will, and emotions)
- a spirit

Each human being is created by God in His image, who is also a three-in-one Being—Father, Son, and Holy Spirit. (See Genesis 1:27.)

In Dr. Rebecca Brown's book *Prepare for War*, there is a graphic of a demon spirit forging, melding, and unifying a link between an individual's soul and spirit.[2] Dr. Brown goes on to explain that this is not the way the Lord created man. Man was created by the Lord in three separate parts: body, soul, and spirit. This melding is not the Lord's will. He wants our spirit linked with His Holy Spirit. Astral projection links the human spirit and soul together to form an astral vehicle that is powered by a demon. The astral projector goes illegally into the spirit world. Dr. Brown further claims that if this demonic link between the soul and spirit is left unsevered in anyone who has been involved in the occult, it leaves an opening to continuous demonic torment from Satan's kingdom, even after deliverances.[3]

Dr. Brown further explains in *Prepare for War* that men's physical bodies are weak and of little use to Satan, but their spiritual bodies, under the conscious control of their souls, are very different. She goes on to tell us that Satan's goal is to teach humans to regain the conscious control of their spiritual bodies.[4] Many do. Once this is achieved, these people can perceive the spirit world as well as the physical world. They can talk freely with demons; they can leave their physical bodies; and with their spirit bodies and with full conscious awareness, they can go places and do things with, what seems to the average human, supernatural power. They can levitate objects without ever touching them physically, light candles without a match, create physical healings, and more. These human spirits can torment and afflict people just the same as demon spirits do.

The Modern Catholic Dictionary defines *bilocation* as "Multiple or simultaneous presence of the same substance or soul in two places distant from each other. Bilocations have been frequently reported in the lives of the saints."[5] This ability to bi-locate has been taught across the U.S. in Catholic lectures according to Dr. Brown.[6]

The "astral world" is the spirit world. Open communication with the spirit world is the goal of all Eastern religions as well as satanism. This is in contrast to the Christian's goal to be led by the Spirit of the living God, not by demons.

> Astral projection is the counterfeit work
> of the enemy and it cannot be done without
> a human operating in partnership with
> the devil and his legions of demons.

Astral projection occurs when a person engages with a demonic entity to such an extent that they turn over the control of their mind, will, emotions, and their spirit to demonic deception and demonic activity. Individuals in astral projection are deceived to believe that by *their own power* and *by their own will*, they can separate their soul and their spirit from their body and transport (astral project) themselves. Self-will is the original sin. Satan said, "*I will* ascend" (Isa. 14:13, emphasis added). These individuals do make a *choice of their own will* to partner up with demonic powers to accomplish this separation of their souls and spirits from their body. Then the individual and the demon travel throughout the earth and universe.

> Translation by the Holy Spirit is for
> Christians such as Philip. Astral projection
> by demonic power is the counterfeit.

Some people argue that astral projection is only a false perception, a dream, a hallucination, or that they travel into the atmosphere only in their minds. Astral projection is the counterfeit to the biblical account of Philip's translation in Acts. Philip was moved for purposes of the kingdom of God from point A to point B by the power of the living Lord and *not* by the power of demons as in astral projection.

Some astral projectors claim they only do "white" or good projection while other astral projectors do "black" or evil projection. This is the same as saying there is a difference between white magic (witchcraft) and black magic (witchcraft). Remember the enemy is a deceiver and a liar, and all astral projection and witchcraft are his work.

The Bible says we perish because of lack of knowledge (Hosea 4:6). It is time that we become aware of such attacks and of such an enemy operating against the church.

> By definition, *astral projection* is "being
> projected like a star into the atmosphere—
> just beyond human perception."

Dictionary definition of *astral*:

> Star or starlike structure; relationship to a star; like the stars designating or of a universal substance supposedly existing at a level just beyond human perception.

Dictionary definition of *projection*:

> Projecting or being projected.

Astral projection is human souls and spirits invisibly or visibly projecting around with the power and partnership of demonic entities.

Further, it is reported that in order to do this it is necessary for the individual's spirit to stay connected to their physical body with their "silver cord." Ecclesiastes 12:6 tells us to "remember your Creator before the silver cord is loosed." Astral projectors believe that if their silver cord is cut while they are projecting out into the atmosphere, they will instantly die and their spirit could be hopelessly lost in dark outer space. That sounds like hell to me.

In Shirley McLain's book *Out on a Limb*, she states, "My spirit or mind or soul, or whatever it was, climbed higher into space. And attached to my spirit was a thin, thin silver cord that remained stretched though attached to my body. I definitely felt connected. What was certain to me was that I felt two forms...my body form below and my spirit form that soared. I was in two places at once, and I accepted it completely....I watched the silver cord attach me to my body.... It glistened in the air. It felt limitless in length....totally elastic, always attached to my body."[7]

The worst fear for an astral projector is to be out on an excursion and have their silver cord cut. The church has the power to overcome astral projectors.

Astral projection is a very real and serious enemy of the church. Isaiah 59:19 promises us, "When the enemy comes in like a flood, the Spirit of the Lord will lift up a standard against him."

In his book *The Unfolding*, volume two, R. B. Edwards portrays the false prophet as an astral projector in the book of Revelation. We meet the false prophet in Revelation 13: 11–18; 19:20; and 20:10.

Revelation 16:13–14 says, "I saw three unclean spirits *like frogs* coming out of the mouth of the dragon [satan], out of the mouth of the beast [the antichrist], and out of the mouth of the false prophet... for they are spirits of demons, performing signs, which go out to the kings of the earth and of the whole world, to gather them to the battle of that great day of God Almighty" (emphasis added). This is the counterfeit, unholy trinity orchestrated by satan. Satan is the father of lies, and the false prophet is the religious mouthpiece of the antichrist. "...the false prophet who worked signs in his [the antichrist's] presence, by which he deceived those who received the mark of the beast and those who worshiped his image. These two were cast alive into the lake of fire burning with brimstone" (Rev. 19:20).

Second Thessalonians 2:9–11 tells us "the coming of

the *lawless one* is according to the working of Satan, with all the power, sign, and lying wonders" (emphasis added). Satan will empower the false prophet to produce deceptive signs and lying wonders among those who perish. Those who don't love the truth will be allowed by the Lord to believe the lie.

This is why we see the huge buildup in our culture, on the Internet and in our nation and the world of astral projection. It is deceptive, powerful, and unholy. It is a tool of Satan to deceive even the very elect, if possible. This is all a buildup to Revelation 13 and the introduction to the world stage of the false prophet. Our defense against being deceived is to love the truth. Jesus is the Way, the Truth, and the Life.

Chapter 2

ASTRAL PROJECTORS' PURPOSES

1. Steal Christians' faith in God by wearing down the saints (Dan. 7:25, KJV)

They:

- Stalk them
- Oppress them
- Harass them
- Depress them
- Cause them to lose hope
- Sabotage them
- Gossip about them
- Accuse them
- Lie to them
- Rape them
- Molest them
- Beat them up
- Steal from them

2. Use Christians like pawns

So the Christians:

- Feel like they are in an eggbeater; are confused; feel they may be crazy and/or mentally insane
- Obsess with: What is wrong? What is going on? What have I done wrong?
- Are hindered continually
- Their plans, hopes, and dreams are sabotaged
- Feel incompetent

3. Target Christians and their families

- Astral projectors meet in New York City regularly to pre-determine spousal changes.
- Their targets are the saints in the kingdom of God.
- Their purposes include: loading down the saints with serial astral projector spouses, and wearing down the saints with discouragement and loss of hope.

4. Target ministries to bring confusion, sabotage, disunity, and ruin

5. Partner with witchcraft networks that stretch over this country like a net

This net is fine—an invisible network of evil.

6. Change values to produce sin and the resulting judgments of destruction and death

Chapter 3

HOW DOES A VICTIM OF SEXUAL ABUSE BECOME A VICTIM OF ASTRAL PROJECTION?

1. They can suffer a failure to discern about their own lives

Because of sexual abuse or other abuse in childhood, they:

- Do not fully trust their Lord
- Do not trust their own hearts
- May have distorted values

2. They were unprotected

Parents and caregivers did not protect their child from the abuse and abuser(s).

3. They were uncovered

Parents and others did not plead the blood of Jesus over these children daily.

Chapter 4

HOW CAN A VICTIM OF ABUSE GO INTO ASTRAL PROJECTION?

A SEXUALLY OR OTHERWISE ABUSED CHILD MAY turn out to be a perpetrator of astral projection and/or a victim of it.

The Lord in His mercy and grace gives natural defense mechanisms to all of us to help us get through difficult circumstances in our lives. This is also true in cases of sexual and physical abuse in children. There have been many reports from adults who said the Lord took them up out of the traumatic event. They would just "check out" or even leave their physical bodies while the abuse was taking place, and this helped them better deal with it and survive it. Some of them report they even looked down and saw what was happening to them below.

The Bible tells us that sin brings death. Many times the child does not tell their parents or another adult about the sexual and/or physical abuse. This can bring demon harassment to the child even into adulthood as long as the abuse is left hidden and until the individual is delivered by the power of the blood of Jesus and the authority of His name.

I believe that children who have been prayed over and covered by the blood of Jesus are protected from going into astral projection. Children not covered by the blood of Jesus, who are victims of sexual or physical abuse, can learn that these God-given defense mechanisms give them *power* over and *safety* from their abuser. It starts by "checking out" so they don't have to experience the abuse. Later they can grow into adulthood practicing this "checking out" over and over until they become adept at astral projection.

People can also innocently get into the deception of astral projection by having "eyes in the back of their heads." It is said that these people seem to have extra sensory perception also known as ESP. Many of them profess to be Christians. They may be deceived into believing that they are only using the gifts of the Spirit. Carnal Christians can cross the fine line and get into ESP in ignorance and deception.

One example is of a woman who knew what was happening with her children half way across the United States. One time when her grandchildren's cat was killed on the highway, the grandmother called her daughter and asked her over and over what was wrong. Finally the daughter remembered that during the previous week the children's cat had been killed. The grandmother stated that she knew something like that had happened. The daughter was troubled in her spirit by this. For years the entire family had known that Grandmother seemed to have "eyes in the back of her head."

ESP is a slippery slope and an entryway into astral projection. Dr. Gwen Shaw has written an excellent book

The Fine Line. This book details the difference between the soul and the spirit. She states that there is little understanding of the difference between the soul and the spirit for it cannot be discerned by the five senses. She further explains that spiritual things must be spiritually discerned and, sadly, there is not much awareness of this in the body of Christ.[1]

We need to listen carefully to the nudgings of the Holy Spirit. He will led believers into all truth if we will listen to Him with our whole hearts. Then we won't have to worry about the legitimate use of the gifts of the Holy Spirit.

These abused individuals who go into astral projection are conditioned and deceived into believing their supernatural ability comes from their own power, which comes from their own choice and will. They do not discern that these powers to astral project their soul or to have ESP is from a demon. Being so deceived, they love the stealth, the power, and the control it gives them. This unholy power is intoxicating to them.

Many in witchcraft who become Christians go back into witchcraft for the same reasons—they love the control and power it brings them. Both astral projectors and those in other forms of witchcraft love the exploits they can do.

Astral projectors mock and scorn the Holy Spirit anointing of Christians and the exploits they do by the Spirit. Projectors believe their power is superior to that of the Christian. This is why Christians must have greater discernment and anointing to overcome astral projection assaults against them. You cannot fight and overcome an enemy you don't know exists.

Individuals who practice astral projection may proclaim they are Christians, but they have no fear of the Lord. Have you ever ministered to someone and they did not change? Psalm 55:19 tells us, *"Because they do not change, therefore they do not fear God."* If the projector believes the lie that his power is greater than the Lord's, he has no fear of the Lord.

Chapter 5

UNHOLY SOUL TIES CAN LEAD TO ASTRAL PROJECTION VICTIMIZATION

In an unholy soul tie, your mind, your will, and your emotions are NOT your own.

SOUL TIES ARE SERIOUS AND ALL UNHOLY SOUL TIES must be broken off an individual. This can be done by repentance on their part and by using the blood and the name of Jesus. Unholy soul ties come from unholy sexual intercourse, from parental abuse, and from agreements with any person who has exhibited unholy control over a person.

I once ministered to a Christian man who had been involved in a great number of sexual relationships. As I was ministering to break soul ties from him, in the spirit the Lord showed me how He saw this man's soul. It looked like a piece of Swiss cheese. This reminded me of the times in the New Testament when Jesus healed people and He would say He had made them every bit whole.

I believe that unholy soul ties are like superhighways for

astral projectors to come in on to harass and unknowingly control, hamper, and stress their victims. Unforgiveness is another superhighway for torment to come into your life. Jesus told us in Matthew 18:34–35 (KJV) that if we do not forgive, we will be delivered to "tormentors." An astral projector interfering in your life is a tormentor!

Sexual or physical abuse can spiral victims into astral projection by taking them over with an unholy soul tie. Compromise to survive can muzzle a person's voice, their will, and their inner person because it has been given over to the perpetrator of rape or abuse. With this compromise the abuse victim's voice is overruled, and the demonic takes over in stealth control. Unconsciously, young victims make inner vows, attachments, appeasements, treaties, and false peace with unclean spirits. Bitter root expectancies put victims in the position of being a magnet of evil, and the individual becomes part of a vicious downward spiral that leads to astral projection, *either as a victim of it or as a perpetrator of it.*

Those with unholy soul ties, pawns of projectors and astral projectors have their real voices overridden and shut down by the demonic. Their "yea" is not yea and their "nay" is not nay (James 5:12, KJV). James also tells us a double-minded man will receive nothing from the Lord (James 1:7–8). Here James is telling us it won't work to have one foot in the Lord's camp and one foot in the enemy's camp. In this state, your faith can be robbed, because you can decree a thing and it does not come to pass even when it is aligned with the Scripture. And without faith it is impossible to please God (Heb. 11:6).

It is said that there is a demonic altar from where demons send out astral projectors to shut down victim's spirits and their voices. With a shut down spirit and voice, it is hard to say the name of Jesus, to praise Him, to worship Him, to pray to Him, and to read His Word with revelation from the Spirit.

Demons, familiar spirits, and projectors are all assigned to sexually abused victims to perpetually keep them pawns through confusion, stress, lack, hindrances, and desolation. Demonic entities can come and go at will. This makes them harder to discern, especially if they have been with a child from an early age. The abused individual does not recognize that it is anything but normal.

These demons can vacate when there is someone around who is praying or has the gift of discernment. They can "check themselves at the door" of the church, so to speak, to keep from being discerned. They operate like "stealth bacteria" that attack the body's immune system by working just under the body's radar. When someone who ministers to an abuse victim does not discern this, the victim can be perpetually trapped in a satanic-orchestrated abyss.

Therefore, the abuse can potentially affect the lifetime of a victim and even their future generations. This gives us greater revelation and understanding of why Jesus said, "It would be better for him if a millstone were hung around his neck, and he were thrown into the sea, than that he should offend one of these little ones" (Luke 17:2).

Many times the church condemns the victim for continuing to be a victim. These pat, trite answers only add salt to their wounds. This scenario applies to those who fight bitter roots of hatred, anger, rage, murder, sexual addiction, homosexuality, self-hatred, low self-esteem, multiple abusive relationships, and astral projection, to just name a few. These roots can stem from childhood sexual abuse and abuse of every kind. The beast is both within and without. The victim's sure hope is to run to the Lord. He will be there with open arms to all those who call upon His name.

Chapter 6

THE FEAR OF THE LORD IS THE BEGINNING OF WISDOM

THE FEAR OF THE LORD IS ONE OF THE SEVEN Spirits of the Lord. (See Isaiah 11:1–3; Revelation 1:4; 4:5; 5:6.)

The Holy Spirit is the third person of the Trinity and is not divisible from the Father and the Son. Therefore, I don't believe one can have the Holy Spirit and yet not have the fear of the Lord. Astral projectors pose to be Christians but they do not have the fear of the Lord. Christ is not divisible. You either have Him in your heart or you don't. Astral projectors could well be in that group of people who say, "Lord, Lord."

Jesus said in Matthew 7:21–23 (emphasis added):

> Not everyone who says to Me, "Lord, Lord," shall enter the kingdom of heaven, but he who does the will of My Father in heaven. Many will say to Me in that day, "Lord, Lord, have we not prophesied in Your name, cast out demons in Your name, and done many wonders in Your name?" And then I

will declare to them, "I never knew you; depart from Me, *you who practice lawlessness!*"

Astral projection is a high form of witchcraft. It is strictly forbidden by Scripture and is rebellion and lawlessness (1 Sam 15:23). Isaiah 33:14 tells us, "The sinners in Zion are afraid; Fearfulness has seized the hypocrites." Astral projectors trade knowing Jesus for the stealth, power, and control the devil gives them. Astral projectors see themselves as strong and able to do great exploits. They are some of the most deceived people on the earth. They are playing into the hand of the enemy. He has them and yet they think they are the controlling ones!

The astral projector's conscience is seared. "Now the Spirit expressly says that in the latter times some will depart from the faith, giving heed to deceiving spirits and doctrines of demons, speaking lies in hypocrisy, having their own conscience seared with a hot iron" (1 Tim. 4:1–2). Their hearts remain uncircumcised. Their minds are not renewed. They cannot have true intimacy with Christ Jesus. They cannot repent without the fear of the Lord and the gift of repentance. They fill our churches doing all the right motions but they can never really receive. (See Jude 12–13.) They may be deacons and elders and some of the best givers, sing in the choir, and lead cell groups in their homes. But they are really clouds without water! The Apostle Paul warned us that after his departure "savage wolves will come in among you, not sparing the flock" (Acts. 20:29).

Chapter 7

TIPS TO HELP SPOT ASTRAL PROJECTORS AMONG US

FIRST AND FOREMOST WE MUST PRAY FOR THE Lord to bless us with more *discernment* and *anointing*. His Spirit will point astral projectors out to us if we are seeking Him. We must seek His face to trust Him more and to also trust what He tells us. Jesus told us in John 10:27, "My sheep hear My voice, and I know them, and they follow Me." We learn to trust that voice by practice and by walking closely with the Lord. When we read His Word, as we ask Him we can expect Him to speak to our hearts from the Word. Then we need to obey from our hearts what He speaks to us.

Some Key Indicators to Help Spot Projectors

1. Do they have the love of the Lord?

First John 4:8 tells us that anyone who does not love does not have the Father and does not know God.

2. Are they being changed from glory to glory?

Psalm 55:19 tells us that without the fear of the Lord there is *no change*.

3. What is their fruit?

Jesus said we can know them by their fruit (Matt. 7:15–18). Does an apple tree produce tomatoes?

4. Do they know Him intimately?

To know Him means that you dwell with Him in the secret place of the Most High (Ps. 91:1–2). This type of knowing is as Joseph knew Mary. It is as a husband knows his wife. The two are one. To know Him speaks of intimacy with Christ. The hymn "In the Garden" speaks of this intimacy with Christ. Written by C. Austin Miles in 1912, he says, "I come to the garden alone...and I walk with Him, and I talk with Him."

This close intimacy with Christ brings about changes in us, transforming us from glory to glory. (See Romans 12:2 and 2 Corinthians 3:18.)

When we are transformed we will have certain characteristics:

- We will show forth the glory of the Lord:

    on our faces

    in our worship

    in our testimony

    by our words

- Our countenance will show His presence.
- We will desire more intimacy with Christ.
- We will love His Word.
- We will be known by our love for the Lord and for others.

Watch Out for These Characteristics— Wolves May Be Among You

They:
- Do not enter into the presence of the Lord
- Do not enter into corporate worship but stay on the fringes
- May call it praise and just be making noise
- Are not free in their spirit
- Do not have a ready smile but a contrived smile
- Seem to be odd and they probably are
- Are argumentative
- Are unteachable
- Are stubborn
- Are divisive, causing divisions and strife
- Quench the anointing
- Have a religious spirit, the spirit of anti-Christ and many other sins that come with it
- Have the spirit of Jezebel, which may mask the astral projector and other sins

- Are controllers
- Are liars
- Seek to be the center of attention
- Seek out pastors and other leaders to befriend
- Seek the glory for themselves
- Lack the love of the Father
- Have no fear of the Lord

True Christians are:

- Unable to be in unity with them
- Unable to share true fellowship of the Spirit with them

Chapter 8

ASTRAL PROJECTION AND OUR CULTURE

Comic Books Can Lead into Astral Projection

Some comic books are full of astral projection. Many people think of comics as innocent childhood entertainment. But many comics have heroes who practice astral projection. Children and young adults who have been the victims of sexual abuse can easily fall prey to the demonic pull toward practicing astral projection from this childhood "entertainment."

Cartoon and Movie Characters Practice Astral Projection

Instead of just reading about astral projection, now you can see it on full color screen where characters with these super powers are made to look intelligent, powerful, and innocent.

Harry Potter Can Lead into Astral Projection

The Harry Potter book and movie series are primers on witchcraft. These books and movies have astral projection throughout them. Yet, these books are touted as good children's literature—to deceive even the elect (Matt. 24:24). One intercessor and leader said, "With Harry Potter, now astral projection is out of the closet."

New Age and False Religious Practices Teach and Promote Astral Projection

The Internet is full of websites about astral projection and out-of-body experiences. It is taught step by step. It has long been a part of the New Age Movement, transcendental meditation, chanting, Eastern religions, witchcraft, and the metaphysical. They all teach astral projection. They claim you have to be "highly evolved and/or enlightened" to have it.

> Our culture has become saturated
> with astral projection.

In reality, it costs a high price. You can lose your soul and hell awaits.

> According to occult teachings the astral plane can be visited consciously through astral projection, meditation and mantra, near death experience, lucid dreaming, or other means. Individuals that are trained in the use of the astral vehicle can separate their consciousness and spirit in the astral vehicle from the physical body at will.[1]

The term *astral plane* has also more recently come to mean a plane of existence where otherkin believe their souls reside.

> Otherkin is the term for a group of people who consider themselves non-human or having a connection to a mythical archetype in some way, usually believing to be mythological or legendary creatures. Common creatures to which Otherkin claim some connection include angels, demons, dragons, elves, fairies, lycanthropes, and extra-terrestrials. The otherkin community grew out of the elven online community of the early-to-mid-1990s, with the earliest recorded use of the term otherkin appearing in early 1996. Outside of their own subculture, otherkin beliefs are often met with controversy...According to diagnosis criteria put forth in the DSM IV and the ICD, the belief that one is an animal or can be turned into an animal may qualify as a delusional disorder...of varying severity and significance. [2]

In *Dungeons & Dragons* planar cosmology, the astral plane is used as a means of transportation between planes, a dimension coexistent with all others. Color pools on the plane lead to the other worlds it touches. The astral vehicle remains connected to the physical body during the separation through a so-called "silver cord" mentioned in Ecclesiastes 12:6.[3]

The astral plane is the final level of the computer game

NetHack. The player must sacrifice the Amulet of Yendor to a deity in order to win. The video game *Windwalker* identifies the astral plane as another dimension through which the Alchemist, one of its characters, can summon demons, influence dreams, and cause evil in the natural world.[4]

A major part of the musical *The True Story of the Bridgewater Astral League* by The World/Inferno Friendship Society is the astral plane. It is also featured in the surreal 2000 comedy film *The Nine Lives of Tomas Katz*.[5]

The astral plane is referenced in popular songs such as "Bring the Pain" by rap artist Method Man, "No More Pain" by 2Pac, Morphine Machine with "Astral Plane" and "Astral Plane Pt Deux," Aerosmith with "Draw the Line," Jonathan Richman with "Astral Plane," and "Dream Weaver" by Gary Wright.[6]

The astral plane is traveled through when astral projecting, reached through orbing, and described as a realm of "spirits and energies" in the television show *Charmed*. It describes eleven planes of existence, including a "ghostly plane" inhabited by the dead before they are escorted to the afterlife by the Angel of Death.[7]

Chapter 9

REAL LIFE ISSUES AND ASTRAL PROJECTION

Astral projectors love the stealth, the power, and control over others it gives them. Business people like astral projection because it gives them a very competitive edge. At a sales leadership conference, I met a man who told me he had unusual high sales among the Amish near his home. At an evening dinner for the company's top sales people he sat right across the table from me and talked "Christian-ease." He talked a lot about angels, but his talk was hollow. I didn't sense the Lord was with him. I even asked him if he was born again. He said yes, but it was a hollow answer, and I sensed that there was something odd about him. The next day he told me he was into astral projection, but only "to do good." He said it was the secret of his sales success. He also told me that astral projection was taught to him in the military. Evidently there are secret military operations that teach our men and women in uniform astral projection to help us win wars.

> People steal your finances and your
> good name by astral projection.

All astral projection is a form of witchcraft. Witchcraft is from the pit of hell and the devil. There is no grey area. We are in a battle, and a lot of our battles come from the powers of darkness.

I know a family that took in an orphan from Jamaica. They entered into a dark and unseen battle, which lasted almost a year and was one of the worst they had ever encountered. It was over the heart, soul, and future of this young man from Jamaica. Mission workers from the U.S., who called themselves Christian, decreed that they were going to blackball the family and their ministry because they were jealous. They wanted control and power over the young man under the guise of helping him. They wanted to use him to raise funds for their own selfish purposes and to receive glory for themselves.

After much prayer, the Lord showed the family in the spirit what this attack looked like. It came from the home of one of the ladies attacking the family from a distant city. What looked like a twelve-inch, round plastic cylinder rose up from her home and went and hit a pastor's home in South Dakota. The cylinder was filled with black, churning smoke. Once it hit the pastor's home, it exploded all that black smoke into a giant black ball that totally engulfed that pastor's home. An intercessor in the family saw that the black smoke originated from hell and was contained in a square room in the home of the distant attacker. From that day on the family lost favor with that pastor and all his contacts on behalf of the orphan. Their ministry lost two board members. They lost many contributions and offerings from the circle of people who were covered with that black smoke. Astral projectors can project all kinds of curses, as well as their souls and spirits. And they can also assign other astral projectors to you.

I have a few suggestions to overcome such an attack. First of all, "having done all, to stand" (Eph. 6:13). Also, shut off communications from the attacker and have no personal contact. Keep your heart right. Don't take up any offense or allow unforgiveness or bitterness to take root.

It is the enemy's plan to get you involved with these attacks from the astral projector and snare your feet in his net of confusion. It is easy to miss the obvious. Get your eyes off the projector and onto the demonic powers behind the projector. We have power and authority over them.

Rise up in the Spirit and in the power and authority of the name of Jesus and render the demons *powerless* that transport the astral projectors. Every time you discern you are attacked, render those demons powerless.

Chapter 10

ASTRAL PROJECTION PROVIDES THE COVER TO COMMIT THE "PERFECT CRIME"

H OW CAN ONE BE CAUGHT OR PROSECUTED when there is no physical evidence? Think about it.

- There are no fingerprints.
- There is no DNA.
- There are no eyewitnesses.
- There is no physical evidence of any kind!

One astral projector bragged to me that he could push someone out of a third-story window and never get caught. He said he has practiced crime for years. All he has to do is keep his mouth shut and not tell anyone and he will never get caught. Another astral projector told me how he had escaped and evaded the police numerous times because he was able to hide by quickly changing his appearance and his identity.

It was reported to me by intercessors that a man practicing astral projection projected himself visibly into the showers of three single women at an international ministry headquarters. All three of these women told me of this and the shame and condemnation it had brought upon each of them because each one of them thought it was from their own evil imaginations. As they confessed their faults one to another (see James 5:16) and compared notes, they learned that the man came through the sin of astral projection and that it was his sin and not theirs.

Another intercessor reported to me that a man known to her from her church was attacking her in her home with his astral projection. While she sat in her living room, she experienced this person pressing up against her in a sexual manner. She also had items missing from her home that were of special importance to her. Often after prayer these items would reappear, although many times the items never returned.

This same man was in good standing in the local church, a Spirit-filled, charismatic church. Intercessors saw in the spirit that this man was astral projecting himself sexually upon women during the Sunday morning church service. Some of these women were on the front row, so this was going on right under the pastor's nose as he was preaching. This happened Sunday after Sunday. The man often appeared to be sleeping during the church services, but he was just sitting there with his eyes closed while astral projecting himself on these unsuspecting women. The women attacked said they knew he had been rubbing up against them sexually during the service, but they could not understand it because they had never heard of astral projection or even imagined such a thing. They felt helpless to stop it, and because of shame they didn't tell anyone for a long time.

One particular attack was upon a middle-aged woman who was a member of that church. She reported that this same man had astral projected himself into her bed at home and had sexual intercourse with her during her sleep. This happened repeatedly. She knew who it was, but she could not prosecute for rape because there was no evidence.

There is always a door open to allow astral projection to have access. This particular church had Freemasons in leadership. I believe that is why the pastor was hindered from discerning astral projection in his church.

I know an intercessor from that same church who was physically attacked twice by astral projection. The first time was as she entered a home for a prayer meeting. As soon as she sat in a chair at the dining table, she was slugged in her stomach very hard by a single fist. There was no one around her. But she knew who did it—her husband! He was across town on his way to counsel with the pastor of the church. He had just dropped her off at the prayer meeting.

The second physical attack to this intercessor came in her sleep. She was beat violently in her sleep one night. She reported she was violently beat in her abdomen by what she described as a two-inch dowel rod with a blunt end. She said it felt to her as if it had been thrust deeply into her guts relentlessly over and over by a very angry person. When she woke up the next morning, she could not stand upright because the pain in her abdomen was so strong. She was doubled over in pain for most of that day. This attack had happened in her sleep and she awoke with the pain and the knowledge of what had happened. She prayed throughout the day about who did it and why. The Lord showed her who did it—the husband of a couple who claimed to be Christian. He was jealous of this family's ministry.

Another intercessor from the northwest told me about her discernment of another man practicing astral projection. He also was in a church service with his eyes closed but not sleeping. The Lord opened her eyes in the spirit and she saw him astral projecting to the front of the church service to interfere with the ministry of the pastor and church leaders. This man was a large giver in the church. His photograph was even on the front of a pamphlet for a northwest Christian retreat. He was pictured kneeling and praying and looked so spiritual in that photo.

This intercessor reported that this same man used to call her often. She was an apartment manager. Often she found that her apartment had been broken into and her files had been gone through with items moved and or missing. The police could not help her because there was no physical evidence. She thought she was going crazy. It robbed her of her peace, her joy, her health, and even her trust in the Lord, bringing in unbelief. Finally she discerned that all of this was coming upon her because of this man's phone calls. When she broke off her friendship with the person, shut off her phone, and moved in with her elderly father half way across the country, her battles stopped.

We must be informed about astral projection and not be afraid to talk about it in our churches. The enemy is already within the gates.

A Jamaican intercessor told me that she saw a man from the U.S. astral projecting down to Ocho Rios, Jamaica, for the purpose of toppling pastors. In the spirit, she stepped right up to him, stopped him, and kicked him out of Jamaica. Then she saw him astral project over to the Dominican Republic and again, in the spirit, she stepped right up to him, stopped him, and kicked him out. For the third time, she said he astral projected to another Caribbean country and she stepped up to him in the spirit, stopped him, and kicked him out. She spoke with authority and real resolve. Jamaica has a lot of witchcraft brought in from their African roots. So the pastors and intercessors there are more aware and able discern astral projectors than the churches in the U.S.

Another intercessor in Jamaica told me that when she was in London she had a boyfriend who was into astral projection and told her a lot of things about it. She had not realized that she was his target until I spoke in her local Jamaica church about astral projection. Before I spoke in this church about astral projection, both of these Jamaica intercessors had kept this information to themselves because they didn't think anyone would believe them.

A Jamaican pastor has given me a lot of information about

astral projection. We befriended him during our month long mission trip to Jamaica in June 2006. Then in the first eight weeks of 2008, the Lord sent him to be a guest in our home. He was an answer to my prayers for more information about astral projection. This is what he taught us:

- The astral projector has to pay money to their demons to keep their powers. The demon requires a specific amount and it *must be paid on time*! The astral projector has to lay the cash in the specific place in their home for the demon to come and pick it up at a set time. This is essential or the demon attacks the astral projector. This is why astral projectors always say they are broke no matter how much money they earn. They can't keep it.

> It is a demon that takes the astral projector's soul and spirit traveling and *rules* in the astral projector's life.

- The astral projector must kill a *family member* with astral projection to gain power. (There is a similar requirement to becoming a witch doctor in Ghana, West Africa. The upcoming witch doctor must kill someone by

the power of his witchcraft to prove himself
a witch. The victim does not have to be a
family member in Ghana.)

- The astral projector has great power, but it is
limited by God.

This Jamaican pastor has an uncle who is an astral
projector so he has had a lot of personal experience with this
subject. When the pastor's younger brother was in school,
his neck was snapped and broken while he was sitting in
his chair and he died instantly. After this uncle murdered
his brother with astral projection, the pastor was stricken
with what the doctors thought was typhoid. But his symptoms were not the symptoms of typhoid. His skin was
turning from jet black to brown and he was dying. Finally
his doctor recognized that he was dying from witchcraft.
Pastor was delivered and healed.

Pastor also witnessed that when an astral projector was
sick and broke and could not pay his astral projection dues
to the demon, the demon attacked him so viciously that
all the neighbors came to see what was happening to him
as he was dying. His meals turned to mush, liquid on his
table turned to blood, and stones were thrown at his house
although no one was seen throwing them.

Pastor told us that astral projectors can turn themselves
into animals, frogs, lizards, etc., to gain access and open
doorways into others' life and property. One intercessor's
thirteen-year-old daughter was terrified when she saw a

black panther coming down the hallway of her parent's home. She said it had red blood dripping from its teeth and that it was looking for her mother to kill her. She saw this twice. That was right after her mother had married a "fine Christian man." He said the daughter was hallucinating.

But other intercessors said the Lord showed them the daughter had seen this black panther in the spirit. This intercessor and her daughter lived another five years with this man. They both got very ill. The mother had serious nosebleeds for months, and it was found that they were being systematically poisoned with carbon monoxide gas. Another intercessor praying for them saw a black panther stalking on the outside of her home. In the spirit a third intercessor saw a black cat jump upon the screen door to the patio to get inside. The panthers and black cats were seen in the spirit before any of these intercessors knew anything about astral projection.

This woman's husband would also quite often imitate a frog. He had a previous wife who had died from cancer. They had all kinds of frogs all over their house. Even the cards they had given each other were frog cards. He would make sounds like a frog and squat down and hop around, all the while twisting his face to look like a frog. She hated it and seemed to know there was something evil about it. But she had never been taught about astral projection and did not recognize her enemy.

Chapter 11

COME OUT FROM AMONG THEM

Come out of her, my people, lest you share in her sins, and lest you receive of her plagues.
—REVELATION 18:4

PERHAPS YOU OR SOMEONE YOU KNOW IS LIVING with or personally involved with an astral projector and is afraid to leave. In their eyes it is not much different than trying to leave someone in the Mafia, a mob, or a gang.

Anyone who has been married to an astral projector knows that to leave will bring on reprisal and retaliation. There is a fierce battle that goes on and they have great fear.

Divorce is always a hard choice. Malachi 2:16 tells us that "God...hates divorce, for it covers one's garment with violence." But how can two walk together if they are not agreed (Amos 3:3)?

My people are destroyed for lack of knowledge.
—HOSEA 4:6

I was told of one woman on the east coast who had divorced an astral-projecting husband and was in danger of losing her home. Intercessors said they had not taken her as seriously as they should have because they just didn't realize how serious her plight was.

Here is the personal story of a woman minister and missionary who was married to an astral projector. (These are not their real names.) The wife, Jill, said that she had known from the start of the marriage that there was something terribly wrong with her "wonderful Christian husband," Tom. For five years Jill had prayed and anguished over what was wrong and how to help Tom. She also suffered guilt about why she wasn't thankful for this "fine Christian man" and looked for ways to be a better wife to him.

Tom had lost his previous wife to cancer. After his marriage to Jill, he moved her and her daughter, Sarah, into his home. Later Tom told Jill that his deceased wife had desperately wanted to move from that house because she felt it was killing her. Tom said that his deceased wife had him move her to the country into a singlewide trailer he had bought. Tom was an industrial maintenance mechanic, so he knew OSHA safety rules. Even so, Tom repaired the double shower stall in the trailer by spreading dangerous levels of epoxy all over that enclosed area. The epoxy pulled the oxygen out of her system, and that low oxygen environment caused the cancer cells in her body to thrive. Shortly after that she went to the hospital and never recovered.

Tom also told his new wife, Jill, that his previous wife had died of a broken heart because none of her daughters or grandchildren ever came to see her during her last days. The family of the deceased wife told Jill that her husband, Tom, had refused to let the family in to see their mother and grandmother. He had told them that she did not want to see her family. Tom kept them apart by his lies. Her family was very angry at him because of this. And thus, a root of bitterness defiled many (Heb. 12:15). The longer Jill knew Tom, the more of his lies were revealed.

Tom also told Jill shortly after they were married that the people in the small town they lived in all thought that he had killed his previous wife. He told her that he was afraid they would try to arrest him. So Tom said he had put a loving tombstone on her grave to dispel their anger.

So when Jill married this "fine Christian man," he moved her into his "nice" home, which they later found had hidden, toxic, black mold in it named *stachybotros*. This was the same house with the mold that brought on the death of his previous wife, and he knew it. Even when Jill and Sarah both got asthma, Tom didn't tell them about the toxic black mold. It was only when Jill's doctor said to look for mold that she found it. Then Tom told his wife, Jill, to report it to the insurance company. The insurance company ordered environmental tests and found the toxic mold. Then, and only then, did Tom tell Jill about the autopsy of his previous wife. They had found that his deceased wife's liver had a very different type of cancer, one which was caused by mold.

Tom and Jill lost their home and all its contents to the toxic black mold. Then they lost a luxury apartment and all their contents to toxic black mold again. Jill got very ill. She had months of illness with seemingly no way out. Her daughter, Sarah, also got very ill.

Still Jill was active in ministry and was an associate minister at a local Spirit-filled church. She knew the Lord gave her that position to strengthen her and give her hope. Jill had counseled with her senior pastor and asked for prayer about her confusion about her husband. Like the others who were victims of astral projection, Jill was concerned that she might be losing her mind. Her pastor assured her she was not losing her mind and that her husband was only in the flesh like King Saul.

Jill realizes now that the Lord led her pastor to mention King Saul because King Saul was not only operating in the flesh but he also turned to a witch for direction and power to bring Samuel back from death to talk to him. In other words, he was involved in witchcraft.

Jill's husband had always interfered with the anointing and mocked it. She reports that Tom had interfered with every sermon she prepared and preached. Every night before Jill was to preach, Tom would confess to her some bizarre sin that would upset her. She had to pray very hard to keep her heart right and keep her anointing to preach after these "confessions." He had no respect for the anointing on anyone. Now Jill realizes that Tom felt that his power of astral projection was stronger than the anointing. He once told Jill that if she wanted to go to a foreign field to do missionary work, she had to fly herself there without a plane. Tom told Jill when she projected herself to the foreign field, she would be ready for missionary work there. Jill now knows he was insinuating that if she did not master illegally entering the spirit world throuh astral projection, that she was not qualified to do Christian mission work. That is arrogant astral projection mockery.

Before Jill separated from him, Tom told her the problem between them was that she was royalty and that he was a commoner. Another time Tom told Jill that she knew a different Jesus than he did. Tom told his wife that he couldn't be intimate with Jesus like she was. Jill reports that Tom was very adamant about once saved always saved. If you are astral projecting, you would have to be adamant about that! I think he was banking on "fire insurance." No matter how much Jill prayed and ministered to him, she could not reach him.

Tom had been in many churches before they were married. Several of those churches suffered church splits. One of the pastors went crazy and lived under a bridge and ate grass for several months. People in their town know about this pastor and what happened to him. No one understood why. I think it was the result of this "fine Christian man's" astral projection.

It was after much prayer by many intercessors that Jill's

"fine Christian husband" confessed to her all about his astral projection. Jill had gone on a trip with her husband and called an intercessor to meet with them early the next morning. She had been praying that her intercessor friend would hear from the Lord and would discern what was wrong with her husband. That night before the intercessor came, Tom admitted to his wife about his astral projection. He told her he could project his soul anywhere! She believes it was the power of Lord from those intercessors that brought about his confession.

Jill reported that when her husband, Tom, confessed his astral projection to her, the picture suddenly became clear. The confusion suddenly left. Her spirit was flooded with understanding and revelation.

After Tom's confession, Jill took the report to her senior pastor. He was shocked and in unbelief. How could such a "fine Christian man" be an astral projector? She told him to ask the church intercessors. He just couldn't believe this church member who was such a good tither could be doing astral projection. Tom was the pastor's good friend. He was in utter shock that such a thing could be happening in his church.

Besides all the spiritual attacks and desolations brought on by being married to an astral projector, there is a specific agenda they want to achieve. Demons are what prompt them. The enemy wants your health, your life, your reputation, your house, your money, your car, your circle of influence, your children, and the destruction of your ministry and your calling, and your greatest treasure—your faith, just to name a few.

Jill believes Tom married her to:

1. Consciously or unconsciously kill her

2. Take over and sexually abuse her daughter in her absence

3. Steal her money—a substantial amount from the sale of her property

4. Stress her continually by his:

    control

    sabotage

    secretiveness

    unwillingness to be in unity

5. Be sanctified by a believing spouse

For the unbelieving husband is sanctified by the [believing] wife.

—1 Corinthians 7:14

Satan knows the Word well and knows how to pervert it. I believe astral projectors target and marry strong Christian spouses whom they believe will protect them in their astral projection and sanctify them.

The believing spouse gets the brunt of the attacks. It is the enemy's agenda to deceive, wear down the saints, and steal their faith. Our greatest gift and treasure is our faith for without faith it is impossible to please God (Heb. 11:6). When the saints are beat down, the enemy of our souls has created the lukewarm church that Jesus will spew out of His mouth (Rev. 3:16, KJV).

We need believers standing in the gap for victims of astral projectors. I know the intercessor who took in Jill when she left her astral-projecting husband. The intercessor prayed the Word over Jill when the attacks intensified. She repeatedly prayed Psalm 35 over her, putting her name in the text and making it a decree over her life. The intercessor continually spoke words of love and hope and encouraged her in the Lord and in life. Shortly after Jill moved in, a prophet came to visit the intercessor's home. He said the Lord showed him that Jill was like a little bird with a broken wing. All that afternoon Jill cried and used an entire box of Kleenex because she knew that was how far she had fallen.

The Lord's economy is always perfect. The intercessor had suffered great personal loss in her life with four deaths of close relatives six months before the woman moved in with her. So they ministered to each other. A close bond of trust, unity, and love bound the two together in ministry. A strong foundation was built in both the intercessor and in the woman minister. The Lord is so good!

You can never out-give the Lord. What you do for others, He will do for you. Now, this intercessor and Jill co-pastor a home church and the Lord brings the deeply hurting to them for ministry. They know it takes time, prayer, the balm of Gilead, love, and fellowship to build trust and mend the wings so the hurt and wounded saints can fly again. The Lord wants to take His people high in the Spirit, into the deep places with Him, under His wings, and into secret places with Him.

Finally, the woman minister has been able to go to the foreign field as a missionary. Together she and the intercessor have taken eight mission trips. The Lord has always showed Himself strong on their behalf, and they have done exploits in His name.

Jill reports that all that kept her alive during those dark days with her former husband was the vision the Lord had given her of ministering on a foreign field. His Spirit and strong arm sustained her to fulfill her vision. She reports she could have easily given up life without that vision from the Lord.

> Where there is no vision, the people perish.
> —PROVERBS 28:29, KJV

The Lord is good and His love is everlasting!

> Astral projection is rebellion against the Lord and man and is a form of witchcraft.

Chapter 12

HOW TO PROTECT YOURSELF AND YOUR HOUSEHOLD FROM ASTRAL PROJECTION

B<small>E HOLY. KEEP YOUR LIFE AND YOUR HOUSEHOLD</small> pure. There is no substitute for holiness. Pray for strength, double anointing, and double discernment. Listen to and obey the Lord. He will speak to you and show you anything in your life or home that displeases Him. Deal with it immediately.

Maybe there is something inside of you such as anger, rage, or resentment. Confess your sins, repent, and turn from your wicked ways. Don't delay. Don't nurse old grudges. Clean them out of your life. Ask the Lord to reveal any hurtful way in you. (See Psalm 139:23–24.)

Jesus said, "Love the Lord with all your heart, with all your soul, and with all your mind. This is the first and the great commandment" (Matt. 22:37–38).

Call on the name of Jesus and plead the living blood of Jesus over yourself, your home, and all of your family members. Do it daily. Do it every time you drive your vehicle.

Cleanse your property if the Lord tells you to. Anoint your door posts and windows with consecrated oil and wine. Anoint yourself and your family members as often as necessary. Walk around the perimeter of your property. Pray over and consecrate the elements of oil, wine, and bread. Sprinkle the consecrated elements on the perimeter of your property. Bury the wine and the bread at every corner and at any place the Lord tells you. Dedicate your life, your home, and your property to the Lord. Make a blood line in the Spirit that the enemy cannot cross.

Decree the Word of the Lord over yourself, your family, your property, and your finances.

Take communion often and prayerfully. Communion means to commune with the Lord. Make His cross your table.

If the astral projector still crosses into your home or property or finances, seek the Lord for why. He will tell you.

One couple was told by the Lord to check their TV remote because a hair had been placed in it as an access point. They obeyed the Lord and found a piece of one strand of hair in the TV remote. Then the Lord told them to check on top of a tall wall cabinet. There taped on top of the cabinet was one strand of hair. This is why we must maintain a close walk with the Lord and listen and obey. Once these two strands of hair were removed, the breach was stopped.

Chapter 13

HOW TO OVERCOME ASTRAL PROJECTOR ATTACKERS

THE NEW AGERS AND THE ASTRAL PROJECTORS tell you they are projecting themselves out by their own will and strength. They do not astral project on their own strength. That is part of the great lie and deception that they live under and proclaim to others. Revelation 20:10 tells us, "The devil...deceived them."

If they were really projecting under their own super evolved strength, and their own willpower, as they claim they do, then we could feel helpless because we cannot take spiritual authority over another person's will. This goes back to the Garden of Eden when the Lord God gave man a choice. He did not stop Adam and Eve from eating the fruit of the Tree of Good and Evil. He knew what their choice would produce, but He let them have free will. This is foundational to our faith.

Consequently, if we buy into the deception that they astral project under their own strength, then we can fall into the devil's trap to try to take authority and control over another person. By doing this, we can easily get into what the Lord considers witchcraft. We have no legal right in the kingdom of God to take someone else's will and choices away, even in what we consider to be righteous prayer. Our Jamaican pastor friend has told us that it is a demon who takes them on their astral projection trips.

Another claim the astral projectors make is that they must stay hooked to their silver cord as they are astral projecting to be able to get back to their physical bodies. In his book, *Journey into the Miraculous*, Todd Bentley gives a testimony that he was ministering to a woman to bring her out of witchcraft and her satanic high priest kept interfering. They gave him much notice to cease and desist what he was doing. Finally, the battle got very intense. Todd and his team gave repeated warnings and the man did not stop trying to prevent the woman from getting delivered and saved. Finally, Todd prayed and asked the Lord to cut the satanic high priest's silver cord. Immediately the man died of a heart attack in a distant city.[1] I believe those who are generals and in the higher ranks in the Lord's army are especially targeted and attacked by astral projectors and witchcraft. The Lord entrusts greater power and authority to them because they are tested and true to His holy character.

Jesus said, "Behold, I give you power to tread on serpents and scorpions, and over *all* the power of the enemy: and *nothing* shall by any means hurt you" (Luke 10:19, KJV, author's emphasis). Astral projection qualifies as a work of the devil! It is evil!

When Jesus sent the seventy out "they returned with joy saying, 'Lord, even the demons are subject to us in Your name.'" Jesus answered, "I saw Satan fall like lightning from heaven" (Luke 10:17–18). So if the seventy disciples had such authority over the enemy that even the head of the wicked, Satan, fell from heaven, then we can have confidence that our prayers to defeat the demons that transport the astral projectors will manifest results.

I have heard two stories about astral projectors (Satan's operatives) falling from the heavens to share with you. First, from Africa there was a report of a naked man dropped out of the sky to the ground *unharmed*. To me that is an example of God's love for that man. The natives in that community knew that he was a displaced astral projector who had lost his demonic power and fell to the ground. So the natives picked up sticks and stones to kill him. The police took him into custody to protect him from the crowd. I was amazed that *the man was naked*. This speaks to me about how astral projectors attack people in their sleep to have sex with them. After Adam and Eve's fall, *they knew they were naked* (Gen. 3:7).

Secondly, another report told of a group of witches who were astral projecting over Africa and got into a fight in the heavens. One of them got knocked down and fell to ground—*again unharmed and again naked.*

We Christians have all power and authority over astral projection. In the name of Jesus and by the power of His blood and the authority He gave us, we can command those demons to be stopped from astral projecting. We have to be led by the Spirit of the Lord in our prayers and must have His discernment in every case. There are no formulas to follow.

Astral projection is not something we should run from or fear. We should be like David who went into the battle with Goliath with his five smooth stones and his faith in the Lord. We must not shrink from the battle. We can win. We have *His* power to win. We cannot turn over our country, our government, our schools, our media, our economy, our legal systems, our churches, our ministries, our homes, or our children to astral projection. We must pray for more discernment and rout out the enemy. For too long this enemy of astral projection has run secretly, bringing desolation, loss, and shame. We need to take up our God-given authority command the astral projector's demons to be powerless and cast out. In John 12:30–31, Jesus said, "...for your sake. Now is the judgment of this world; now the ruler of this world will be cast out." This applied to satan as ruler of the world system (vv. 31; 14:30; 16:10), ruler of demons (Matt. 12:24 and Mark 3:22); and ruler of the air (Eph. 2:2). He is a defeated foe. Astral projectors are deceived pawns operating under a defeated foe.

In Isaiah 61:7 the Lord promises, "Instead of shame you shall have double honor." Job got double back all he had lost (Job 42:10). The Lord promises that He will give you double for your trouble. He is no respecter of persons (Acts 10:34, kjv). If you have been storm tossed and greatly afflicted, just know that the Lord sees, He is your defender, and His glory is your rear guard. None of this takes the Lord by surprise. He knew before the foundation of the earth that we would see this day when the church would be so assaulted. He tells us that He has given us the power to overcome.

There are many rewards to those who overcome. See Revelation 2:1 through 3:21.

> And they overcame him by the blood of the Lamb, and by the word of their testimony; and they loved not their lives unto the death.
>
> —REVELATION 12:11, KJV

We can overcome any enemy with the Word of the Lord and the blood of Jesus. Jesus spoke the world into existence, and at the end with only the Word from His mouth, He will defeat every enemy. Revelation 19:13–21 tells us that the Lord is the Word of God and a sword will come out of His mouth to strike the nations.

Read and declare Psalms 23, 35, and 91 out loud. The Word of the Lord is powerful, more powerful than any enemy.

John 10:10 tells us, "The thief does not come except to steal, and to kill, and to destroy." When a thief is caught he has to pay back seven times what he stole. Proverbs 6:31 (KJV) tells us, "If [a thief] be found, he shall restore sevenfold; he shall give all the substance of his house." Enforce this word against all the work of the enemy if you have discovered he has stolen and taken from you because of astral projection and witchcraft of all forms. If God be for us, who can be against us? Jesus won the victory on the Cross, there is no weapon formed against us that will prosper.

Chapter 14

HOW to SET CAPTIVES FREE FROM ASTRAL PROJECTION

YOU OR SOMEONE YOU KNOW CAN BE SET FREE from astral projection by the Word of the Lord, the name of Jesus, and the power of the blood of Jesus. They must have genuine repentance and turn from it.

- You will need keen discernment to minister to astral projectors.

- They may *say* they have stopped doing it, when they have not.

- Beware of their lying; it is second nature to them.

- Know that they will be trying to control and manipulate you.

- Beware! They know all the right things to say; they know "Christian-ease."

- They know all the right ways to act.

Witches are known to come to deliverance ministers only to have their easily discerned, "lesser" demons removed from their lives. Satan is well versed in the Bible. He knows Luke 11:24–26: "When an unclean spirit goes out of a man…he goes and takes with him seven other spirits more wicked than himself, and they enter and dwell there; and the last state of that man is worse than the first." Witches go to churches for prayer so they can get more demons and become stronger witches. Beware of the wiles of the devil (Eph. 6:11)!

Discern, Discern, Discern

After much prayer, the Lord showed me that He sees the astral projectors' spirits and souls as *kidnapped* by demons. Astral projection is done in agreement with demonic power.

Astral projectors falsely claim *they* project their souls and that *they* keep themselves hooked to the earth by their silver cord. But man's silver cord is tied to his spirit. Ecclesiastes 12:6 tells us that at death the silver cord is loosed. When Jesus died on the cross, He *gave up* His spirit. Astral projectors' spirits and souls both are projected by demons.

> Astral projectors are deceived because
> astral-projecting demons have held captive,
> kidnapped, bound up, and tied together
> the projector's soul and spirit into one
> unit and project out both together.

The astral projector's soul and spirit bound and tied together is contrary to how God created man in three distinct parts—body, soul, and spirit.

An astral projector with a kidnapped, captive, and bound-together soul and spirit has a lot of demonic limitations:

> Astral projection is the UTMOST rebellion against the Lord and against His creation because it is against the image of God in man. Astral projectors deceive others, but they are the ones who are most deceived. They came into agreement with astral projection, but they did not bargain for *their soul and spirit to be kidnapped and held captive.*

- A projector cannot have a close, personal, and intimate relationship with Jesus because their spirit has been held captive by the astral-projecting demons. Astral projectors can be around the most anointed people and ministries, read their Bibles, talk the Christian language, and are still unable to receive or have a deep, intimate relationship with the Holy Spirit, Jesus Christ, and His Word.

- Although astral projectors can use Christian gifts because the gifts and callings are without repentance (Rom. 11:29, KJV), they walk as divided people and are split into more than one personality. That is why we can see some people flow in ministry and, on the other hand, participate in witchcraft or astral projection.

- A bound, held-captive projector cannot share their soul or spirit with their spouse or family. Their relationships are shallow and unfulfilling due to a lack of intimacy because their soul and spirit have been kidnapped by demons.

Dr. Rebecca Brown has had good success in setting the captives of witchcraft and astral projection free.[1]

1. She relies on the living Word of the Lord in Hebrews 4:12 (emphasis added): "For the Word of God is quick, and powerful, and sharper than any twoedged sword, *piercing even to the dividing asunder of soul and spirit.*" Dr. Brown believes the victim must repent and ask the Lord to remove the demonic link and divide between his soul and spirit according to Hebrews 4:12.

2. Next, Dr. Brown relies on 1 Thessalonians 5:23 (emphasis added): "And the very God of peace sanctify you wholly; and *I pray God your*

whole spirit and soul and body be preserved blame-less unto the coming of our Lord Jesus Christ." Note that these are listed as three distinct and separate parts of the human being that need to be sanctified.

3. Then one must cry out as David did with his whole heart. "Create in me a clean heart, O God; and renew *a right spirit* within me" (Ps. 51:10, KJV, emphasis added).

Chapter 15

STEPS TO FREEDOM FROM ASTRAL PROJECTION

Get with a pastor or an intercessor who understands astral projection and holds you accountable to walk it out. You must be mentored in all honesty by godly men and women with keen discernment.

- You must desire with your whole heart to rebuke, renounce, and resist your demonic power and all astral projection.

- You must be willing to admit that you have been deceived into believing that your astral projection is by your own soul power.

- You must admit, confess, renounce, and repent that you have been astral projecting by demonic power and deception.

- You must come to terms that you have been deceived at the very core of your being.

- You must *choose* to be delivered from the demonic hold and deception it has on you and your mind.

- You must *repent* and turn from it entirely. You need to pray for the gift of repentance from the Holy Spirit.

There may be a part of you that is not willing to give this up and surrender it and your life to the Lord. This is a stronghold in your mind. This will be a struggle that you and the Lord can win if you are willing to pay the price to lay down all the demonic power and control you have been using for years.

The Bible tells us in 2 Corinthians 10:4–5 how to win these battles:

> The weapons of our warfare are not carnal but mighty in God for pulling down strongholds, casting down arguments and every high thing that exalts itself against the knowledge of God, bringing every thought into captivity to the obedience of Christ.

Get gut-level honest with the Lord. *This is not something you can do yourself.* Only the Lord can set you free. Pray an honest prayer and ask Him to give you a willing spirit (Ps. 51:12, NIV), and to grant you a willing spirit to sustain you. Call upon Him with your whole heart, mind, and soul, and He will answer you.

> Therefore if the Son makes you free, you shall be free indeed.
>
> —JOHN 8:36

You could spend eternity in hell. Don't play games with your future address.

Today He has set before you *life* or *death*. Choose life!

> I call heaven and earth as witnesses today against you, that I have set before you life and death, blessing and cursing; therefore choose life, that both you and your descendants may live.
>
> —DEUTERONOMY 30:19

NOTES

Chapter 1
What Is Astral Projection?

1. Definition and information on astral projection found at http://en.wikipedia.org/wiki/Astral_projection (accessed April 22, 2009).

2. Rebecca Brown, M.D., *Prepare for War* (New Kensington, PA: Whitaker House, 1987, 1992), 164.

3. Ibid.

4. Ibid.

5. Fr. John A. Hardon, S.J., *Modern Catholic Dictionary* (Bardstown, KY: Inter Mirifica, 1999), s.v. "bilocation."

6. Brown.

7. Shirley McLain, *Out on a Limb* (New York: Bantam Books, 1983), 327–329.

Chapter 4
How Can a Victim of Abuse Go into Astral Projection?

1. Gwen Shaw, *The Fine Line* (Jasper, AR: Engeltal Press, 1985).

Chapter 8
Astral Projection and Our Culture

1. Information from the article on astral plane, http://en.wikipedia.org/wiki/Astral_plane (accessed April 27, 2009).

2. Information from the article on otherkin, http://www.answerbag.com/q_view/119602 (accessed April 27, 2009).

3. Information from "The Astral Plane in Popular Culture," http://en.wikipedia.org/wiki/Astral_plane (accessed April 27, 2009).

4. Ibid.

5. Ibid.

6. Ibid.

7. Information on the TV show "Charmed," http://en.wikipedia.org/wiki/Charmed (accessed April 27, 2009).

Chapter 13
How to Overcome Astral Projection Attackers

1. Todd Bentley, *The Journey into the Miraculous* (Shippensburg, PA: Destiny Image Publishers, Inc., 2008).

Chapter 14
How to Set Captives Free from Astral Projection

1. Brown.

BIBLIOGRAPHY

Bentley, Todd. *The Journey into the Miraculous*. Shippensburg, PA: Destiny Image Publishers, Inc., 2008.

Brown, Rebecca. *Prepare for War*. New Kensington, PA: Whitaker House, 1987, 1992.

Edwards, R. B. *The Unfolding*, vol. 2. Victoria, BC: Trafford Publishing, 2007. This novel is a work of fiction based on the prophetic outline of end-time events. It reveals the Book of Revelation in an easy to-understand presentation. The author references the False Prophet as an astral projector on pages 18 and 100 with an introduction to him on pages 15 and 16.

Hardon, John A. *Modern Catholic Dictionary*. Bardstown, KY: Inter Mirifica, 1999.

McLain, Shirley. *Out on a Limb*. New York: Bantam Books, 1983.

Shaw, Gwen. *The Fine Line*. Jasper, AR: Engeltal Press, 1985. Gwen Shaw is the founder of End-Time Handmaidens.

ABOUT THE AUTHOR

Rev. Marilyn Schrock is an ordained minister of the gospel from Christ for the World International under Apostle Bobby Hogan, Ft. Smith, Arkansas, and Global Network Ministries under Dr. Rob Carman, Red Oak, Texas. She is also a member of End-Time Handmaidens, Jasper, Arkansas. She attended Christ for the Nations, Dallas, Texas, in 1985 through 1987. She graduated with a Juris Doctorate in 1996 from Washburn School of Law, Topeka, Kansas. She is listed in the 2007–2008 Madison Who's Who of professionals, New York, New York.

In 2005 Rev. Schrock founded a not-for-profit organization, The Potter's Hands Inc., along with a church, The Potter's Hands Church, in Emporia, Kansas. She also founded The Potter's Hands, a non-profit organization in Jamaica. She has led eight mission trips to Jamaica.

In 2006 Rev. Schrock brought home Kevin, who was just released from a state run orphanage in Jamaica. Before Kevin came to the U.S. at age nineteen to be Rev. Schrock's son, he had only two and one half years of formal education. Within two years he received his GED and is now in his second year of college with a B+ GPA. Rev. Schrock has three other grown children and five grandchildren. Her calling is to teach the body of Christ who they are in Christ, to set the captives free, and to preach the gospel to the poor with signs and wonders following.

To Contact the Author

jamaicamarilyn@aol.com

www.WakeUpChurch.com